7 Secrets to Becoming An ELEGANT Lady

Lady Jeannette Mack

2022 Lady Jeannette Mack

Printed in the USA (Print Version):

No part of this book may be reproduced, scanned, or distributed in any printed, mechanical, or electronic form (including recording or photocopying) without written permission, except in the case of brief quotations embodied in critical articles or reviews.

All content, including text, graphics, images, and information contained or available through this book, is only general information.

All rights reserved for translation into foreign languages.

Printed in the United States of America

Table of Contents

Table of Contents 3

Introduction 5

EXCELLENCE 13

LOVING 39

EXPECTANCY 49

GROWING 55

ATTITUDE 73

NOTEWORTHY 85

TRUSTWORTHY 95

Recap 103

About the Author 107

7 SECRETS TO BECOMING AN ELEGANT LADY

Introduction

Hello, my name is Lady Jeannette Mack. For over forty years, I have focused on what it takes to be considered, accepted, and received as an **ELEGANT Lady**. Over the years, I have had the honor of meeting countless women, both professionally and personally, and many of them have complimented me about my appearance and asked me how I maintain it.

After a while, I realized that I kept giving the same tips and offering the same advice, so I decided to write a book about what it means and what it takes to become an **ELEGANT Lady**. I hope you find this information helpful as you embark on your **ELEGANT** journey.

ELEGANCE encompasses every aspect a woman brings to the table to display her character, content, and creation. Women are unique creatures created by God to enhance the male experience and the family dynamic. From birth, all of us are given specific input that helps determine the direction and destiny of our future. A woman has a unique and special place in that destiny. She brings forth new creations into the world in the form of children. Her Nature is to nurture.

However, she is also a creator and a co-creator. Let's be honest--everyone has free will and can exercise it however they feel fit. And many women unintentionally create an atmosphere that is not conducive to their dreams being met. They aren't aware of the power they have. They don't fully understand the value they bring to the table.

I know that the current trend suggests that all women are Queens. You've seen the memes: "All Women are Queens." "Straighten her Crown." "Queen of my own Kingdom." While the idea of universal Queendom is a noble thought, the reality is that all of us will not be a Queen. By definition, a Queen rules the kingdom. Unless they're talking about being the Queens of their own Queendom (i.e., their own home or family), Queen is a title reserved for royalty and only a few are crowned. But that royal concept can be considered from another perspective. A kingdom is a specific geographical area. The most effective way to be considered royalty, or someone of significance, is to become an **ELEGANT Lady**.

I grew up in Omaha, Nebraska. Although it wasn't the most significant city, it was big enough for me. In elementary school, I was ridiculed and shamed about stuff I wasn't in control of. A few of my peers even laughed at my body's biology as I was becoming who I would be. I was uncomfortable with the feeling, so when I was sixteen, I began working on developing myself into an **ELEGANT Lady**.

I was unhappy about what I saw when I looked at myself in the mirror, so I began to transform myself in a manner that was more to my liking. As the changes became noticeable, boys became interested in me and wanted to be around me.

These were the golden teenagers: boys whose parents were taking care of them, allowing them the freedom to grow up rude, disrespectful, and not intentional about their lives.

As I matured and they began looking at me as if they'd never seen me before, and my initial reaction to the attraction was Dissatisfaction. I soon recognized that I could not measure my self-worth based on the stares of every boy who walked by and made snide remarks.

Women often go through life frustrated and upset that they cannot fight off the reality of unwanted male attention. They question their self-worth and internalize the negative comments, which often keep them from moving to the next level of life they seek. Despite the circumstances, an **ELEGANT Lady** always has a plan, goal, or focus for what she wants to become.

With the newfound physical and personal development more guys started trying to talk to me. Although some just guys wanted to talk to me and be my friend, I soon realized they all of them didn't just like me because I was a wonderful person. They were mostly interested in the physical pleasure that their immature lusts imagined my adolescent body could provide for them. I soon entered into a negative mindset, caused by the constant attention and advances from these boys trying to take advantage of me.

Have you ever wondered what makes a person do what they do? Of course, you have. We all have. As a young **Lady**, I wondered why I was burdened with the types of things I was dealing with. Why did I have to deal with hand-me-down clothes, not having enough money, being skinny, and having damaged skin? At the time, I felt like I was being punished, and the punishment would never end. I constantly asked God: "Why Me?" God answered back and said: **"Why**

not you? Because you've gone through that and because you have thrived through that, you can teach other young women how to do the same thing and learn how they can become ELEGANT Ladies and not compromise their integrity or their esteem."

In this book, I will explain the **7 Secrets** of becoming an ***ELEGANT Lady***. Although many of the qualities I describe are universal and can benefit both women and men, my focus for this book is to share my perspective as a woman speaking to and empowering other women. Please do not criticize or question the fact that I'm championing the cause of the value of being a traditional woman. Women are unique and special but are often devalued and made to feel less than their true worth. This book is my attempt to correct that. As an Ambassador of Truth, I want to help rectify that situation. I want to uphold the importance of women being women.

7 SECRETS TO BECOMING AN ELEGANT LADY

This is not only my personal story but includes insightful information about how to see yourself as ***ELEGANT*** and help others see you that way. How to become an ***ELEGANT Lady***. The **7 Secrets of an ELEGANT Lady** are:

1. *EXCELLENCE*
2. *LOVING*
3. *EXPECTANCY*
4. *GROWING*
5. *ATTITUDE*
6. *NOTEWORTHY*
7. *TRUSTWORTHY*

As you read it, I hope you will be encouraged to embrace your own unique ***ELEGANCE*** and become a part of the ***ELEGANT Ladies* Movement**—a community of women who are adopting, learning from, and duplicating the model of my life pattern to become ***ELEGANT Ladies***.

7 SECRETS TO BECOMING AN ELEGANT LADY

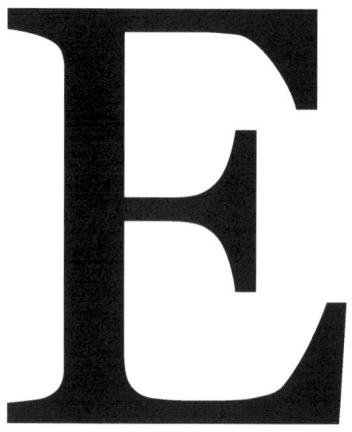

EXCELLENCE

The 7 Secrets of an *ELEGANT Lady*

The first Letter in the word ***ELEGANT*** is "E" for **EXCELLENCE**. EXCELLENCE is a word that is bantered about, and everyone has their own definition of what it means. However, for this book, the definition of EXCELLENCE that I will proceed with is: *Doing your best at all times.* When a woman is convicted to always be and do her best, the result is EXCELLENCE.

First and foremost, an ***ELEGANT Lady*** operates from a position of EXCELLENCE. EXCELLENCE means doing your very best and using everything at your disposal to accomplish your goals, hopes, and dreams.

Comprehending EXCELLENCE from an **ELEGANT** position is crucial. I don't want to diminish it or make light of it. EXCELLENCE is the beginning standpoint of everything worthwhile and valuable. When you approach life from a position of EXCELLENCE, you evaluate what it means to validate yourself. That means you accept and approve of it because it is essential to who you are.

The primary result of doing things to the best of your ability is that you will continually improve and get better. The saying, *"The way you do anything is the way you do everything,"* is a popular phrase that's tossed around, especially in the business world. In her book of the same name, **Suzanne Evans** (who went from being a secretary to running a seven-figure business) explains that you must have the simple determination to excel in everything you do. In other words, everything that you do is all that you do.

Most average and ordinary women don't push themselves to be better. They are content to **"*go with the flow*"** and give the excuse of "being comfortable" over taking a few extra minutes to enhance their appearance to look their best. They wave the banner of "I'm just being me" or not caring what someone else thinks to condone their lackadaisical attire and unwillingness to change. This relegates those women to just being Basic.

On the other hand, an ***ELEGANT Lady*** operating from a position of EXCELLENCE will intentionally get up early, so she has adequate time to make sure that she always looks her best. She's intentional about her hair, wardrobe, skin, makeup, and the image she's projecting to the world. She always looks pulled together, even when she's not leaving the house. She recognizes that image is everything and that you never get a second chance to make a first impression. An **ELEGANT Lady** never walks out of the house wearing a bathrobe or slippers. She ensures that the face she presents to the world, is the face that she wants the world to see.

EXCELLENCE does not mean perfection; you are human and will make mistakes. But you can overcome those mistakes and become better despite them. EXCELLENCE implies that you are willing to give your all and then some. It means you are ready to go the extra mile to achieve your dreams.

"The Essence of Excellence"

A personal standard of EXCELLENCE includes always doing everything that's required, plus a little more. Like an extra pinch of sugar in a sweet potato pie that little bit more is the "Essence of Excellence." For me, it required that I endure and overcome some hurtful things as a young girl and young *Lady*.

They were not situations that were unique to me. I know that other women have gone through their own challenges when they were young, and some may still be carrying emotional scars. I hope to encourage women to overcome their pasts as I overcame mine.

As I entered puberty, I developed acne, and that, coupled with hand-me-down clothes and living in Market Rate Housing...well, you can see I was facing a lot of adversity at a very young age. As a result, I had to deal with a lot of negative energy, which was mostly my fault. The truth is, I wanted more than our family finances could provide at the time. I wanted more.

Thankfully, I was never bullied or shamed by groups, but a few individuals gave me a hard time. I did my best to handle them immediately. The critic I had to deal with the most was me. I recognize that I've always been stubborn; sometimes, that trait can be fierce and laser-focused. I decided early on not to tolerate bullies, braggarts, or gossips. Junior high and high school kids can be pretty cruel, especially girls. I knew that some girls talked behind my back, and even though their words hurt, I acted oblivious to them. In my solitary world, they didn't exist. I was focused entirely on my future and developing my personal attributes, which later became the foundation of my becoming an **ELEGANT Lady**.

Yes, some days I endured shaming, ridicule, and negative talk as I went to school. However, instead of causing me to get bitter, those incidents propelled me to become better. What initially looked like stumbling blocks became character-building blocks on my path to becoming an **ELEGANT Lady**.

I decided to work on bettering my life by taking a job. After having several summer jobs, I finally landed a year-round babysitting job that paid well, and the family was so awesome. The house was in a lovely part of town, and I was treated like one of the family. It was like I hit the Great Teen Job Jackpot! Having that job allowed me to earn money to purchase some of the things **Emerging ELEGANT Ladies** like. For me, it started with buying Lip Gloss.

> *LIP GLOSS helped me to Believe that I too could Become an ELEGANT Lady!*

The Lip Gloss Story

My mother, Alberta, was the first **ELEGANT Lady** I ever met. She was a wonderful and wise woman, and even with little formal education, she was still one of the smartest people you will ever meet. But being a single mother to eleven children was undoubtedly a difficult task.

She faced many challenges to provide what we needed, and she often even gave us some of what we wanted. She ensured we were presentable in public; our clothes were always clean and pressed, even though they were not the styles and trends other kids wore. Nevertheless, at twelve years of age, I felt like my whole world had ended. Compared to my classmates, I felt like I stuck out like a sore thumb.

The truth is, although I was a very obedient child, I felt alone. I thought I was plain and unattractive compared to my siblings and peers. But "Bert" was beautiful, and she instinctively taught me character traits that ultimately became the **7 Secrets**. I treasure her lessons, and I have abided by them ever since. I think that somehow my mother sensed my feelings of despair, so one day, she took me shopping.

With eleven children, you can best believe we couldn't all go shopping together. I chose to spend a lot of time with Mom, so I would often go shopping with her. Most of my siblings did not desire to go on those trips because they required work, and we seldom got anything out of it for ourselves. So, they figured, "Why bother?" On the other hand, I always enjoyed having that one-on-one time with my mother.

This one particular day, Mom and I were shopping, and she announced, **"Jeannette, I think it's time for you to start wearing Lip Gloss."** I was so excited, and I remember the two of us carefully perusing the myriad of colors until we found the perfect shade.

I was happier than I had ever been, and I could not wait to get home to try it on. Once I did, I experienced a Major Transformation. I looked in the mirror and fell in love with myself all over again. Not the arrogant, snobby, stuck-up stuff I saw in some exhibited by some girls at school. No, the real Self-Love, where you no longer hate how you look. I loved who I saw smiling back at me.

I was transformed by what I saw in the mirror. I no longer saw someone I didn't like. I began to see myself as attractive and worthy of the attention of others. **That tube of Lip Gloss made me feel like a princess.** I began to carry myself with confidence, grace, and glory. I no longer listened to nor tolerated the people that laughed at me. I no longer felt completely vulnerable. I now saw myself as valuable. I believed that I was more than "good enough."

When I returned to school the following year, I was different; my life had completely changed. I eventually went to a dermatologist and got control of the acne. Once I found employment, I could afford clothes, hair appointments, makeup, and so much more. The Lip Gloss gave me Confidence, Courage, and Candor. I started to speak up for myself and to control how people treated me. My very demeanor demanded respect and admiration. I learned what it meant for me to be my best. I learned what it meant to display EXCELLENCE.

During high school, I signed up for and completed a modeling course. I was still very shy and introverted, and the class helped shape my values and self-confidence. In fact, my initial concept of the **ELEGANT Lady Mindset** (which I will expand on later) began there. A few years later, I took another stab at modeling. By that time, I was married and had three daughters of my own. A friend got me an interview, and I was everything the company wanted...except I was too shy and introverted. Unfortunately, over the years I had learned to shrink back rather than step forward with the confidence and courage I'd previously displayed.

I did not get that modeling job, but I did receive a much-needed wake-up call. I realized that I had to operate more in the image of an **ELEGANT Lady**, which meant I had to step into my personal power, even if I was afraid.

Let me tell you, I was scared to death at that point in my life. I had married the man of my dreams. My husband has always been larger than life, and I knew I had to up my game if I was going to keep him. I knew I needed to offer some substance, not just try to get by on my good looks. I began to work on myself, and consequently, I inadvertently created what was to become the mantra I live life by and that I taught my daughters to live by. And I have been blessed to share my wisdom to help hundreds of ladies discover their inner **ELEGANCE.**

An **ELEGANT Lady** has dreams...BIG dreams. She has made the decision to pursue her vision. When she recognizes her **ELEGANCE** and realizes her significance, she will be able to demand and command the things she wants out of life. This is the beginning of the Mindset of EXCELLENCE.

A Mindset of EXCELLENCE means that if given choices or opportunities, you will gravitate toward uplifting goals that will help you reach dreams that you have preset for yourself. Sometimes when people observe an **ELEGANT Lady** only from the surface level, they may assume that she is snobbish or stuck up. She may come across as distant or aloof, but she is not being arrogant.

She is simply displaying her self-confidence and the wisdom she's received about protecting valuable things, including herself. She understands her value and refuses to hide it or put it under wraps. Her EXCELLENCE demands that every aspect of her being is controlled by one singular focused mindset. **"To be the best".**

Being the best means being prepared and focused on achieving your goal. It requires you to make a conscious effort to set up your life to win. On a practical level, it means that you get your rest so that you are prepared to deal with what comes day by day. It means you surround yourself with people who can speak into your life and distance yourself from those who don't. It means that you develop your mind to consistently improve your performance in every area of your life.

Competition is not out of the question for an **ELEGANT Lady**. But it must be chased with a degree of **ELEGANCE** and sophistication befitting her. Unfortunately, it has been a long-standing view that women have the reputation of being "catty" and fiercely competitive with each other. Those negative connotations can sometimes cause women to hold back their personal desire to achieve more. An **ELEGANT Lady's** competitive spirit stems from the idea of EXCELLENCE. Its foundation is the idea that she can be the best she strives to be.

Too often, women are given opportunities to excel, yet they don't push themselves to do more. Instead, they allow themselves to be caught up in and dragged down by the intricacies of life and wonder why they're not getting ahead. They're not getting ahead because they're not pushing themselves hard enough. In many cases, someone who aspires to go higher finds herself not reaching her goal because she's not operating from a position of EXCELLENCE.

A woman gains more when she knows what she wants. She must know precisely what she is striving for. Rosa Parks said: "Stand for something, or you will fall for anything. Today's mighty oak is yesterday's nut that held its ground." A woman without focus will fall on her face. However, when an **ELEGANT Lady** has that focus in mind, that picture, that image in mind, then she can attack it and pursue it with EXCELLENCE.

That EXCELLENCE means that as an **ELEGANT Lady**, she always puts her best foot forward. It means that when she leaves to go to the grocery store, work, church, or any place outside her home, she represents herself as an **ELEGANT Lady**. That may mean she takes extra time to prepare because an ***ELEGANT Lady*** stays prepared so she is never put into a situation where she needs to get prepared!

That preparation means that she ensures that the image she carefully cultivated can be maintained and celebrated. She demonstrates EXCELLENCE by spending the extra time to ensure that her attire reflects the occasion she's attending. It's shown by her appropriate makeup application, ensuring that it enhances her inner beauty and is not overdone to produce a clownish effect.

Now, I'm not suggesting that the only way to dress, apply makeup, or wear your hair is in a way that I would approve of. On the contrary, every woman has a unique style that she confidently presents to the world. When done with EXCELLENCE, her personal style can overcome many of the barriers she faces. But most importantly, when operating from a position of EXCELLENCE, she's making sure she's leveraging every bit of her Talent, Time, and Treasure to position herself to win.

So, what does winning and EXCELLENCE have to do with being an **ELEGANT Lady**? Even children know that winning is a result of doing their best. As a young **Lady** maneuvering the high school experience, I observed that many girls were smart and in a class by themselves. Some were pretty, and they were in a separate group. Often the girls that were physically attractive or had family financial blessings to make themselves popular (trending with the right clothing and hairstyles) didn't work as hard to get good grades as a young girl with less money that had a dream and a vision.

That young **Lady** buckled down and studied when she didn't have to, despite her friends who tried to persuade her not to. She understood and had insight into what would benefit her the most and enable her to start faster and advance quicker. She took courses, volunteered, and gained insight, information, and influence. Finally, she found herself in a position to start realizing some of her dreams. Even in high school, she wanted to win. She was operating in EXCELLENCE.

Alternately, many of the young ladies that I went to school with, from stories I'm hearing even today, all too many young ladies thought that they would be able to get by for the rest of their life on the fact that they were cute, popular, or trendy. Inevitably, the rude awakening came, and they soon realized that the marketplace required more.

In the business marketplace, we are paid in direct proportion to the value we bring. I began recognizing that pattern early on and endeavored to bring as much value to the marketplace as I could. That meant pushing myself to do better, to know more, learn more, and achieve more.

All of that was under the umbrella of EXCELLENCE. Excellence doesn't mean that you are perfect and have no faults or never fail. What it does mean is that you will try, that you will strive, that you will endeavor, and that you will do all you possibly can to reach the mark, the goal, and the targets you set for yourself. It means that, no matter what, you always strive to do and be your best.

So, an **_ELEGANT Lady_** looks at the position of EXCELLENCE with excitement in her mind, her voice, and her demeanor. She recognizes that since she knows her value and carries herself and operates from a place of EXCELLENCE, she can achieve whatever she desires. She sets her standards and boundaries high because she is an **_ELEGANT Lady._**

When I'm in someone's company, I always make sure that they recognize that I operate from a standard of EXCELLENCE. Because I'm aware of the types of clothing that best accentuate my body, the quality of my clothes, and how I style my hair and makeup all help me present my best self. People around me immediately see that I'm presenting and doing my best and perceive me as an **ELEGANT Lady**.

Unfortunately, some women think they have to expose their bodies in a vulgar or tasteless way to be fashionable or accepted. But an **ELEGANT Lady** operating from a position of EXCELLENCE knows she is setting a standard that becomes what others strive to reach.

Early on, I learned to avoid certain clothing items (fad shoes, skirts, dresses, and pants) because I knew another fad would take its place by the end of the season. I learned to buy quality pieces and add them to my wardrobe because quality pieces will always be in fashion and last through several seasons. And they will always look amazing. Quality is a critical element of the Mindset of EXCELLENCE. It means that you will buy the things that will have the best long-lasting effects for you. It displays that you love who you are.

Self-love is **ELEGANCE** in action. It is not being selfish or self-centered. Instead, it's being self-appreciative and taking care of yourself because you recognize that no one will ever take care of you the way you do. The Bible tells us that we should love our neighbor as we love ourselves. Individuals that don't like other people generally do not like themselves. When we operate from a position of EXCELLENCE, we will not only like ourselves but also love ourselves.

As we are looking and striving to reach higher heights and more exciting levels, it is essential to know that we are doing it with a Mindset of EXCELLENCE. Throughout my life, I have worn many hats; mother, employee, and entrepreneur. And in all those roles, I have strived to make sure that everyone I encountered knew that I was a woman of EXCELLENCE. From the time I was a child up until now, I have observed that certain women were treated with respect, and others were trivialized. I was determined to become one of the women that would be treated with respect and admiration. As I incorporated the **7 Secrets** into my life, I started to be recognized as and referred to as an ***ELEGANT Lady***.

When you operate from a process and a position of EXCELLENCE, people learn not to approach you with less than their very best. You inspire others to aspire to be better because your standards, and the standards you allow others to interact with you with, suggest and demand EXCELLENCE.

That EXCELLENCE means you look like a Million Dollars when you step out of the house. Not that you try to overdress or over-impress, but to make sure that you stand out in whatever environment you are in. Not stand out so that people point, laugh or ridicule you like you're the butt of the joke. No, stand out so that people will say, "That is an ***ELEGANT Lady***." A mindset is a presence, and it begins with you having a Mindset of EXCELLENCE.

This mindset says you can reach whatever goal you want because you have the Confidence, Courage, and Candor to do so.

The **ELEGANT Lady** may display her **ELEGANCE** by entering a room. Upon arrival, her main objective is to ensure that those in the room note her boundaries and understand that she is to be respected and not disrespected. Her demeanor demands that when she walks into a room and sits down, people automatically gravitate toward her and begin to treat her a certain way. Moreover, that demeanor is developed from a position of her EXCELLENCE. So, if she takes shortcuts with her grooming, attire, skincare, and other things that matter, she always ends up short.

EXCELLENCE says: "take no shortcuts." Spend the extra time to take care of your skin, spend the extra time to eat right, and always eat good foods. Spend the extra time to ensure that you are "ready for prime time." Make sure your personal branding isn't exposed negatively. Take the time to make sure that when people see you, they see someone of significance and be honored. Take the time to guarantee that they see your **_EXCELLENCE_**.

7 SECRETS TO BECOMING AN ELEGANT LADY

An ELEGANT Lady operates from a Mindset of EXCELLENCE. What are ways you display your EXCELLENCE?

1:_____

2:_____

3:_____

4:_____

5:_____

L

LOVING

Of the many Secrets an **ELEGANT Lady** has, the "L" for **LOVING** is perhaps the most endearing. You see, the quality of LOVING is something that is mythical and, at the same time, physical. Love can cover a multitude of your errors and mistakes, and the Bible says it also covers a multitude of sins (1 Peter 4:8).

The Secret of being a LOVING woman is what makes an **ELEGANT Lady** so unique. To be a Loving woman, you first must accept, acknowledge, and approve of yourself. Before you can LOVE your enemy or neighbor, you have to love yourself (Mark 12:31). The Bible tells us as much, and while this is not a book about the Bible, the biblical principles still ring true.

As I was thinking about this chapter, I was very excited because of two distinctly different dimensions. On the one hand, LOVING is about what you give, the essence of yourself, and your completeness. On the other hand, LOVING is about what you can share with others and how you can bless their lives because you chose to be of benefit to them.

As I mentioned in the first chapter on operating in EXCELLENCE, operating in LOVE has a uniquely different but profoundly powerful process on the self-care platform. An **ELEGANT Lady** who is LOVING wants to be a blessing to others as well as herself. She "*Chooses*" to operate in a LOVING manner, allowing everyone around her (including her opponents and haters) to benefit from her peace, contentment, and general good demeanor. That demeanor results from the LOVING Nature that she possesses deep within herself.

We live in a time when everyone talks about self-love and how important it is to love yourself.

> 7 SECRETS TO BECOMING AN ELEGANT LADY

Nevertheless, they do things that are diametrically opposed to LOVE or affection for themselves. I have discovered that if a woman doesn't love herself, it's impossible for her to love someone else. To be able to LOVE another person, despite their flaws and yours, allows you to gain their trust and favor. The prospect of loving yourself, of self-love and self-care, is remarkable.

Growing up, I realized how unkind and cruel one young lady was toward a hopeless young girl who had no control over what her parents could afford to buy her. Imagine being ridiculed for your skin, clothes, physical features, image, and makeup--all things out of your control. But when she finally gained control, she seized every opportunity to change and subsequently learned how to LOVE herself.

That young **Lady** was me, and I remember the frustration, anger, and hurt I felt when I was teased. Growing through that awkward time is bad enough without someone pointing out for everyone to see that you weren't the cool kid.

I have experienced firsthand the internal impact of negative ways, words, and treatment from others, which I was able to both internalize and destigmatize it. Otherwise, it could have wounded me beyond repair. I have reached out to too many young ladies that have experienced this and worse. Some of them are scarred for life. I learned to Love myself early own. My mother taught me the value of being myself. My tormentor's harsh and unkind words were not enough to cause me concern. That seems from Loving myself enough to ignore those that don't have the privilege of knowing me. (Not arrogant, just convinced lol)

I learned to maneuver around the essence of that Nature, but it never, and I mean never, left me alone. I felt bitter and angry because of how they treated me. Kids have no idea how devastating their teasing and criticism of another helpless student can be. Often the child is scarred for life. But my stubborn Nature wouldn't allow their actions to break me. Even though I felt it was unfair and still felt resentment toward her for treating me that way, I learned to ignore her and focus on being me. I was unable to change or deal with the circumstances of my family's situation at that time. I just made the best of it and kept moving forward.

But even then, there was a LOVING Nature within me, and the **Emerging ELEGANT Lady** part of me said that I needed to LOVE myself so that I could LOVE them. I learned to look within, what I once saw because of acne, I now found beautiful.

When she looked and laughed at my clothes, I realized that my clothes may not have been trendy, but at least I wasn't overweight. I already possessed a body many of them wanted, but God had gifted me with it. I was already an **ELEGANT Lady in Waiting.** Often, we must have a revelation of who we already are in order to position ourselves to advance into an **ELEGANT Lady.**

7 SECRETS TO BECOMING AN ELEGANT LADY

I have heard story after story of young ladies who were treated negatively by their peers. They may have been disrespected, kicked about, downcast, and demeaned. Children can be cruel, and parents and teachers should always support and defend any child that says she is being bullied. But the stories I like to read tell the message of the young **Lady** that survived that negative behavior plus more and yet is still thriving. That is the mantra of what an **ELEGANT Lady** is.

It begins by first learning how to LOVE yourself, gifting yourself with true self-love. You cannot give what you do not have. Self-love enables you to intentionally extend your LOVE to others. Loving them will help them get past their own trials and tribulations. Having a LOVING Nature is essential because the LOVE you extend to yourself becomes the LOVE you extend to others. It allows you to give and positions you to receive.

An ***ELEGANT Lady*** realizes she must have a LOVING Nature because not having it results in having a bitter, regretful, mean-spirited Nature that has no place in a growth-oriented woman. She chooses to LOVE because she values who she is. An ***ELEGANT Lady*** feels comfortable in her own skin and at the same time helps others to feel comfortable in theirs.

The time of high school bullying and competition is well over, and as an ***ELEGANT Lady***, you now get to choose the environment you put yourself in. When you operate from a position of EXCELLENCE, it allows you to make that choice. It is critical that you make that choice from a place of LOVE, one of LOVING yourself enough that you will make sure you do what is best for you. You will eat what is right for you and dress in a manner that displays the more excellent Vision and Version of who you desire the world to see.

As an ***ELEGANT Lady***, you operate with **EXCELLENCE** to do everything decently and in order. As an ***ELEGANT Lady***, you operate out of a system of **LOVE** to demonstrate that you genuinely appreciate others and love yourself. Therefore, you can love others and bless them.

Those are the type of attributes that an **ELEGANT Lady** can lovingly display. The next step is to have a posture of EXPECTANCY.

An ELEGANT Lady has a LOVING Nature
Share some ways you have a LOVING nature

1:_____

_____

2:_____

_____

3:_____

_____

4:_____

_____

5:_____

_____

E

EXPECTANCY

The next Secret is found in the "E" in *ELEGANT* is for the word *EXPECTANCY*. Unfortunately, too many women endeavor just to live life the way life comes at them. In many cases, they lack energy or enthusiasm and have a carefree indifference marked by half-hearted efforts. On the contrary, an *ELEGANT Lady* operates from the standpoint of EXPECTANCY in every aspect of her life; she always expects the best. Certain things are expected of women, and if we operate within those parameters, we can have a life befitting the dreams we set for ourselves.

7 SECRETS TO BECOMING AN ELEGANT LADY

An ***ELEGANT Lady*** always expects the best. She sets boundaries and creates barriers to assure that she is only surrounded by that which is good and people that think well of her. She sets boundaries and limitations so that people will know how to treat her because she expects to always be treated with dignity and respect.

Women often become frustrated and angry when people (especially men) cross unknown barriers. If a woman has set a barrier, but there's no warning that the barrier is there, that may lead to ineffective communication. An ***ELEGANT Lady*** sets boundaries, sets standards, and protects her visibility so that the right person knows those standards and barriers are in place.

Interestingly, people find themselves looking at her barriers, looking at those circumstances, and wondering why they are obligated to abide by those rules. An ***ELEGANT Lady's*** EXPECTANCY creates an accountability system and a measurable marketing system.

To expect the best in every circumstance is not asking for too much. Instead, it's asking for just enough because to accept less than the needed amount is frustrating at best. So, as we move along the spiral that is the foundation of EXPECTANCY, we have to quickly understand what we're trying to achieve.

When you know what you want, it's easier to see what's required of you to receive it. The **ELEGANT Lady** is laser-focused on her goal. She knows where she wants to go and what it will take to get there. She is willing to employ everything needed to reach her destination. EXPECTANCY points her finger at the set point and works toward achieving it as quickly as possible.

So, it's easy to see why EXPECTANCY is such an integral part of this growth process. Being an **ELEGANT Lady** is more than just sitting around in nice clothes and taking advantage of the opportunity.

No, it means having a Goal, Vision, and Dream and creating systems and processes that ensure her expectations are met. Any woman can be an **ELEGANT Lady** if she commits to following the process, but the process requires her to operate from a position of EXPECTANCY.

Having a Mindset of **EXCELLENCE** and operating from a position of **LOVING** creates an **EXPECTANCY** that allows her to imagine beyond what she can currently see. And she is willing to partner (both personally and professionally) with others who not only support her as a person but who also function from a place of EXPECTANCY. The **ELEGANT Lady** sees the future and is willing to share the journey with others who share that same vision.

7 SECRETS TO BECOMING AN ELEGANT LADY

Are you EXPECTING to be received and perceived as an ELEGANT Lady? Share some ways you show EXPECTANCY

1:_____
_____
_____

2:_____
_____
_____

3:_____
_____
_____

4:_____
_____
_____

5:_____
_____
_____

7 SECRETS TO BECOMING AN ELEGANT LADY

G

GROWING

The next Secret is found in the letter **"G"** in the word ELEGANT. The **"G"** is all about an ***ELEGANT Lady* GROWING?** I believe GROWTH is the key element for any viable living being, especially human beings, and more importantly, an ***ELEGANT Lady***. Of the **7 Secrets**, the attribute of GROWING is the singularly most important secrets to her success.

Growth means that you have a mindset of not staying stagnant. When you are stagnant, you become stale, which means that you are of no value or have a lowered value. I will take a moment and talk to you about the Human Value Ladder.

An **ELEGANT Lady** understands her value in the marketplace. Men see her and want to approach her, but many won't because she creates an energy that lets them know she is not that type of **Lady**. As a High-Value **ELEGANT Lady**, she realizes that she must set standards and barriers that are acknowledged and accepted by those she encounters.

Let's be clear: a High-Value Woman, an **ELEGANT Lady**, intentionally decides not to associate with Low or No-Value men. She's looking for a High-Value individual who understands that he must bring something to the table to be able to sit and have a conversation with her because she is an **ELEGANT Lady**. How she accomplishes this expression is very important. She must do it with class and grace. If she does it in a capricious, snarky, or just downright rude way, men will perceive her as not being an **ELEGANT Lady** but being a "B" word.

7 SECRETS TO BECOMING AN ELEGANT LADY

As I mentioned earlier, as an adolescent, I was once ridiculed by an older classmate. She had a job and was able to buy fashionable and trendy clothes. For some reason she decided to point out the fact that I wasn't in style. Although my clothes were clean and pressed, they were not name brand or "Cool". At the time I was going through puberty and had developed a pretty severe case of acne. My hair was okay, but okay is never the standard for an **ELEGANT Lady**. My makeup looked below standard because my skin care was out of control.

The first step was to see a dermatologist for the acne. Once I got my skin under control, my whole demeanor changed and came to life, I began to see myself differently. Soon I was getting new attention from boys and men. I was developing into a young Lady. Next I secured a job and made sure that I did not squander the resources. I intentionally bought select items of clothing that enhanced my look. Also, I got the proper medication and nutrition, so that my skin began to glow and was no longer a negative trait for me. I began to make sure that my hair, nails, skin, makeup, and clothing reflected on the outside my image of myself on the inside.

For me, that represented GROWTH. You see, at one point, I was at a level that I did not want to be. As a **Young ELEGANT Lady,** GROWTH required me to intentionally move beyond where I was stuck, to face what was making me feel unhappy, and be willing to make necessary changes. To find true happiness an **ELEGANT Lady** realizes that happiness is an extrinsic value. It happens outside of you. An **ELEGANT Lady** decides to have a say in what happens to her, thus dictating her own happiness.

That is one of the lessons I hope you learn from this book--GROWTH is essential and must be intentional and continuous. It means always getting better. Each day you wake up is a new opportunity, another chance to advance and to become a better version of yourself. All too often, women stay stuck because they don't realize that they have the capacity, the ability, and the responsibility to make sure they reach the goal they set. They allow the Lower Demons to control their Nature and control their Higher Angels. As **ELEGANT Ladies,** we strive for our Higher Angels to control our narrative, our Mindset, our Brand-Set, and our GROWTH.

So, what does that GROWTH look like? Ultimately, that's the correct question. I learned over time that an **ELEGANT Lady** must ask the correct questions if she wants the correct answers. People are often misguided and get off track because they are asking the wrong questions. Once a question is asked, it opens the door for an answer to come. If that answer is not congruent with a woman's core values, she will not accept it. Even if it is true, the truth won't outweigh how she feels, and she will deny the truth to justify the decision she made.

GROWTH requires that we get better; that we see the situation, have a goal in mind, and most importantly, that we strive to reach that goal. GROWTH means doing whatever it takes to become a woman capable of achieving that goal.

The GOALS Mindset is one of an **ELEGANT Lady's** most valuable assets. It states that you do not have to stay wherever you are. A GROWTH Mindset says that if you focus on something and take action toward that something, Massive Imperfect Action, you can achieve it.

Brian Tracy, one of the business mentors I follow, said: "You can't hit a target that you can't see." More importantly, he said that you must become the woman that you're striving to become. In other words, you can't continue being who you are if you desire to operate at the next level. Your responsibility is to research and define precisely what it is and whom you want to become at this level. When you have a clear picture in mind of exactly who she is and who you want to become, you can take steps to get there. Those steps are what I call GROWTH.

7 SECRETS TO BECOMING AN ELEGANT LADY

For GROWTH to occur, you must be willing to do an honest self-examination in six different areas:

- **G**oals: What goal do you have in mind?
- **R**esources: What resources do you need to reach that goal?
- **O**ptions: What options are available to help you achieve that goal?
- **W**isdom: What wisdom is needed to become the Best Version of your Vision?
- **T**ransition: To get unstuck.
- **H**abits: To get you where you want to be.

Once you have completed a candid introspection, you will be qualified to advance toward the position you are striving for. Brian Tracy said that it is not becoming a millionaire that's important, it's what you had to become to become a millionaire. In other words, the lessons that you learn from self-reflection will leverage you to become the ***ELEGANT Lady*** that you desire to be.

There are four types of people that bring value to the marketplace. I would like to share what those types are so that you can understand the capacity of an **ELEGANT Lady** to receive or not receive someone based on the type of value they bring to the marketplace. That is not a negative; instead, that is a positive statement. The **ELEGANT Lady** knows precisely what her desires are. She knows that she must become a woman who cannot only define her goals, but also visualize her goals and achieve them.

The first type of person that brings value to the marketplace is the No-Value Person. They come with their hand out: asking, wanting to receive, but are incapable or unwilling to give. They choose work that is of little to low value. They are of no value to the marketplace and minimal or no value to the people around them. Why? Because they only are there to take. They are unwilling to give their time, talent, or treasure to ensure that the situation or circumstance is improved.

That continues with the concept of GROWTH that I shared earlier. A GROWTH Mindset in an **ELEGANT Lady** says that you want to bring value. You're not always wanting to take just so you can have something, but you are willing to give back through your time, talent and treasure. In contrast, the No-Value Person often thinks that they have the capacity to be with a High-Value or a higher value individual. They are delusional by believing they deserve an **ELEGANT Lady**.

The second person on the Value Ladder is the Low-Value Person. This person is possibly the most subtle because they are doing something and bringing some value to the marketplace, but not as much as they think they do.

The Low-Value Person is an insidious threat to the whole ecosystem because they don't push themselves or are not intentional about their progress. They are not operating in EXCELLENCE, nor are they operating in LOVE with EXPECTANCY and GROWTH. So, they do not realize that they only bring a meager amount of value to the table.

In business, rewards are based on how much value someone brings to the marketplace. If there is a problem or situation that needs to be handled, a person's ability to provide a solution determines their value in the business. Similarly, in relationships, what you bring to enhance the economic structure and the influence of that relationship is the amount of value you bring to the personal marketplace.

If a man enters the personal marketplace and his credit is shot, he has no job prospects, or he's working a low-paying job, is in debt, and trying to pursue a relationship with a High-Value woman, it causes chaos. The chaos occurs because she, as an **ELEGANT Lady**, has set standards, and if he is not able to meet those standards, then he doesn't meet the criteria of who she's looking for in a relationship. This is not to say that a woman cannot adjust her standard based on the character and quality of the man. But because they are on different rungs of the Human Value Ladder, it will be difficult for them to be on the same page.

The third person on the Value Ladder is a High-Value Individual. A High-Value Person has done all they could, should and would do to get better and position themselves when they find themselves in positions they don't desire.

They paid attention in school and were deliberate about the classes they took. They made the right choices, better choices, and clear choices to prevent them from getting stuck with situations requiring other undesirable choices. GROWTH means that to become a High-Value Person, a person brings appropriate value to the marketplace, the relationship, and every situation they find themselves in.

This High-Value Individual is an individual that is sought after. That doesn't mean that those who have not attained the High-Value Lifestyle are less than them. It just means that they need to strive harder to be able to achieve their goals so they can be considered High-Value individuals as well.

The fourth person in the Human Value Quadrant is the Most Valuable Person (MVP). This is a person that brings tremendous value to the marketplace. They may not have the resources, but they use their skills, talents, abilities, and gifts to leverage themselves to a higher place; a better tier. They are the ones that provide leadership, structure, and direction to a particular situation. They arc intentional about operating at the highest caliber possible. The caliber of EXCELLENCE.

They understand that GROWTH is a necessity, and that they have to continually improve every day, in every way. That person who is the MVP has mastered all that and is now operating at an MVP level. They provide leadership, motivation and inspiration--whatever is required to take the team, the group, the company, or the relationship to the next step, the next iteration.

One of the best examples of an MVP is the late Kobe Bryant. I am not a sports fan, but my husband is, so I studied Kobe's life. I found that he worked twice as hard as everyone on the team. He was the first to arrive at practice and the last to leave, and he would continue practicing long after his teammates had left. He was a High-Value Person, but he continued to grow, to get better and better...gooder and gooder.

That perseverance catapulted him to a higher performance level than anyone else on the team. Although they all had superior elite athletic ability, the fact that he had honed, prepared, and practiced equipped him to operate at peak performance. And that's what the MVP brings to the table.

The Low-Value, No-Value, and High-Value Person all aspire to be the MVP. But they are unwilling to put in the additional time and practice required to move to the next value level. An **ELEGANT Lady** realizes that if she comes to the table with a High-Value Mindset, she will be able to accomplish all of her dreams and more.

Operating as a High-Value Person lets the **ELEGANT Lady** perform at a level beyond her peers and competitors. With this GROWTH Mindset, this High-Value, high achieving woman can now continue her goal and continue to get better, therefore leveraging her prospects and opportunities.

An **ELEGANT Lady** follows the best possible course to GROW. She believes that, because of the boundaries she sets and the obstacles she's overcome, she has the capacity to operate in the arena of success that she's selected and chosen for herself. Her altitude is infinite. The sky's the limit!

Are you GROWING every day to be received and perceived as an ELEGANT Lady?

1:_____
_____
_____
_____

2:_____
_____
_____
_____

3:_____
_____
_____
_____

4:_____
_____
_____
_____

5:_____
_____
_____
_____

A

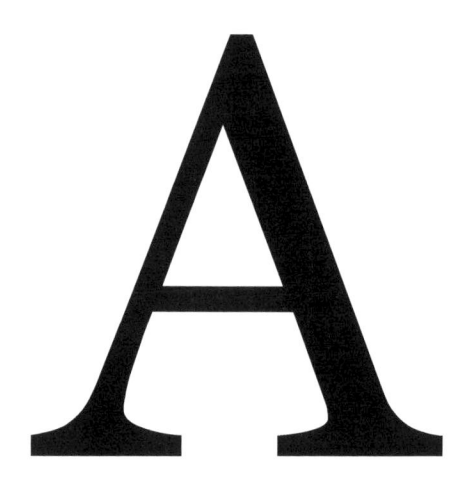

ATTITUDE

The next Secret of an *ELEGANT Lady* is the "A" for ATTITUDE.

A wise man once said: "Your ATTITUDE determines your Altitude." I couldn't agree more. You see, the way you think and the actions you take are the embodiment of your ATTITUDE. How you look at things, and perceive and receive things is an aspect of your ATTITUDE. Your ATTITUDE is the mood and the emotional consideration you give to an event or situation. All too often, your ATTITUDE is skewed by what has happened, what has occurred (your past), or what is currently happening or occurring. It is an emotional display of an inner experience. It is how you express your feelings toward that event or situation. ATTITUDE encompasses all that and way more, yet the **ELEGANT Lady** looks at it from another standpoint. She constantly asks herself: "What is the next best action to take?"

An **ELEGANT Lady** realizes that there are some circumstances that she should not react to. On the contrary, she should respond. To react means that she meets one action with another action. To respond means that she takes considered, deliberate action toward a specific end point or end goal. Her emotional expenditure will show whether she is responding or reacting. The **ELEGANT Lady's** goal is to always continue her image of integrity by fighting the temptation to react and always taking the time to respond appropriately.

I have learned that in life people have trigger points, things that cause them to react. The trigger could be people, places, or things, but the truth is that there is an automatic reaction that occurs. So, when you see this person or hear a certain thing that triggers you, you will react and do a pre-planned thing. The thing that you do quite often is negative when it's caused by a reaction. Triggers release actions and activities contrary to our core beliefs.

Our ATTITUDE stems from the Acceptance, Approval, and Acknowledgment of our Core Beliefs. Our Core Beliefs were developed out of the habits and the input of others early on. Our teachers, parents, and relatives poured into us and set us on a path of thinking, believing, receiving, or having a perspective from a particular discipline or specific direction. Many of the ATTITUDES that we hold were formed not by our own initial intentions but by the deliberate attention of others, such as our parents and other significant others that were allowed in our circle or sphere of influence.

So, we develop our ATTITUDES based on our expectations from our interactions with people, places, and things. An **ELEGANT Lady** establishes the ATTITUDE of EXCELLENCE from the beginning. She also comes from a position of LOVE which allows her to be able to overlook a lot of flaws. She's not searching for perfection, but instead for the person who is trying to do their very best, not just in marriage relationships, but in all relationships: family, career, business, church, community, etc.

So, the ATTITUDE is stacked like a habit, and habit stacking is what we do over time to reinforce the decisions and the actions we make and take. An ATTITUDE is an emotional display of how we feel at any given time. What's your ATTITUDE? In any given situation, that's the question we should all ask ourselves.

Ursula K. LeGuin, a celebrated author, said, "The only questions that really matter are the ones you ask yourself." As **ELEGANT Ladies**, we must ask ourselves: "What is my ATTITUDE, and what has created or predicated it being predominant in my life right now?"

ATTITUDE can come from the fact that as a High-Value Woman, that is an **ELEGANT Lady**, I set standards and parameters that preclude certain people from coming into my inner circle or getting close to me. That's not out of spite or snobbishness, but it's out of a healthy respect for myself.

Recently, my husband, Dr. John L. Mack, designated a Self-Appreciation Day (SAD) due to his observation that most people do not appreciate themselves. "Too many people are unable to like, trust or love others because they don't care for themselves. The Bible tells us to 'Love our neighbor as we love ourselves.' The problem is we don't love ourselves enough." Some people might feel that it's an Ego Trip to want to take care of yourself or to think highly of yourself. I think it is an Idiot Trip if you don't. You must have the ATTITUDE that you are quality and that you are of value. At the same time, you must be humble enough to say that being valuable doesn't make you better than others, but says that you may have made better choices.

As we discussed in the last chapter, our value is predicated on the amount of value we bring to the marketplace and the number of problems we can solve. Whether we get angry or accepting, whether we get frustrated or focus based on what life throws at us, determines the degree to which we have control of our ATTITUDE.

Our ATTITUDE expresses itself negatively due to emotional immaturity. But it expresses itself positively when we make choices and take chances that lead us toward our higher good or greater destiny. An **ELEGANT Lady** realizes that her ATTITUDE will shift her to a higher altitude.

The right ATTITUDE will overcome a multiple amount of errors. An ATTITUDE of entitlement, selfishness, or superiority will turn most people off. And yet, many people walk around with a sense of entitlement. Their ATTITUDE is that the world owes them something just because they're here.

One of the worst things to see is a woman with a nasty ATTITUDE in how she treats people and deals with things. On the surface, it may appear that she is in control, but upon further observation, you'll see that she's fearful and has no control. Therefore, she takes advantage of and manipulates the situation to gain some sense of control. That lack of control causes her to continually strive for something more, never receiving peace or contentment for what she's achieved. That is not to say that we should settle for anything. But it does mean that we should realize that we're entitled to nothing and that everything must be earned. That we are qualified to bring more value to the marketplace.

An ***ELEGANT Lady*** understands her value and strives always to do her best. According to the Bible, a Proverbs 31 woman is a woman that brings all of these elements together in such a way that she's pleasing to her spouse, her children, her family, and to God. She is diligent about her work, loving and caring to her family, and controls her ATTITUDE. She is by no means a "Doormat" for others to walk on. She is intentional about her actions and realizes that she must "Run the Castle, in order for her King to rule the Kingdom"

Controlling your ATTITUDE will continue your ascension toward a higher altitude. Those that are satisfied with mediocrity, with average, with ordinary will find this book to be a little bit intimidating. Yet those who know they have a higher value and are willing to create the atmosphere and the environment to achieve will embrace the attributes I've outlined and apply them to their lives.

Settling is not an ***ELEGANT Lady*** quality. Settling says that you are not going to push yourself; you refuse to operate in the element of EXCELLENCE. That you are not going to continue on the path to GROWTH. That you are satisfied with where you are, the level you are, and that your EXPECTANCY is for nothing more. That is not the characteristic of an ***ELEGANT Lady***.

Because her standards are so high, the ***ELEGANT Lady*** is often misunderstood as someone that has an ATTITUDE or is possibly entitled. Entitlement and Expectancy are two totally different positions. Entitlement says that I should have it because I want it, and I think that I deserve it just because I'm here. Expectancy (which we discussed in a previous chapter) says, "I've done everything with ***EXCELLENCE***, ***LOVE***, ***EXPECTANCY***, with a ***GROWTH*** Mindset, and the right ***ATTITUDE***. And because I have, I expect positive results to come back."

The law of cause and effect allows us to expect specific end results. "If we do this action, then this will occur." If the desired result is established and etched in stone and that pattern becomes reality, then it's possible to allow the ATTITUDE to direct us toward the altitude that we want to achieve.

7 SECRETS TO BECOMING AN ELEGANT LADY

Do you have the ATTITUDE every day to be received and perceived as an ELEGANT Lady?

1:_____
_____
_____
_____

2:_____
_____
_____
_____

3:_____
_____
_____
_____

4:_____
_____
_____
_____

5:_____
_____
_____
_____

7 SECRETS TO BECOMING AN ELEGANT LADY

N

NOTEWORTHY

The letter "N" in *ELEGANT* stands for NOTEWORTHY. So, what does it mean for an **ELEGANT Lady** to be NOTEWORTHY? She is a woman that people take notice of. She's a woman that carries herself in such a way that it causes other people to pay attention. Not that she's engaging in outlandish or performance actions, rather, she's engaging in such intentional action that those around her take note and realize that she doesn't have to follow the crowd to be considered outstanding, she just stands out!

In the Bible, Ruth met her Boaz because she was NOTEWORTHY. Even in a position where she wasn't at her very best, she carried herself with

EXCELLENCE and as an **ELEGANT Lady**. So even as she was gleaning in the fields, she was of such character and quality that it caught the attention of the owner of the field. To be a NOTEWORTHY **Lady** means that you take actions that people notice. Your actions and activities are of such quality and Nature that influential and impactful people not only take notice of them, but more importantly, take notice of you as well.

An **ELEGANT Lady** carries herself in such a fashion that she is noticed. Nowadays, women oftentimes present themselves in such a way that everything is displayed and nothing is left to the imagination. An **ELEGANT Lady** understands that she doesn't have to display all of her wares and her secrets. She can just show up and because of the very Nature of her mindset and brandset, she sets herself apart and set standards that those around her will acknowledge and note as valuable.

How you show up in the marketplace is of tremendous importance. As stated earlier, an **ELEGANT Lady** makes sure that she willingly and consistently does things that other women find annoying or even distasteful. She spends the extra time to make sure that her skin is clean because it's the largest organ on her body and does so much for keeping her body healthy. She takes extra time to either personally groom her own hair or have it managed at a salon.

The clothing selections that she makes are age-appropriate and event appropriate. She doesn't show more than she needs to be able to get the attention that she desires. She dresses not to the point of over embellishment, but to the point of making sure that she does well enough to make the point.

Because she aspires to be NOTEWORTHY, she's intentional about the actions she takes that will get her noticed. To come into public with private intimate body parts showing certainly gets attention, but is it the attention you crave? You see, many **ELEGANT Ladies** have a really unique issue. They get noticed because they carry themselves at such a high level and have such a high degree of EXPECTANCY. That attention often causes people that are not willing to play and operate at her level, to become resentful toward those that do.

Read That Again

Like everything else, being NOTEWORTHY comes with a cost. Esteemed author, Joan Didion, said: ***"Anything worth having has a price."*** As I mentioned earlier, as a young girl in school I was bullied and ridiculed by a mean spirited older girl who had a job and a bit more access to resources. But because I have a mindset and a focus of being a **Lady** of quality, an **ELEGANT Lady**, from early on I strove to create that image. Not in a superficial, fake, phony, or inauthentic way. But in a way that expressed my intent to follow a procedure that was duplicable.

That bears further unpacking. You see there's the proven way and there's the shortcut. I learned a long time ago that a shortcut is the longest distance to the success you're seeking. Often when a female is blessed with tempting attributes such as voluptuous body, hair, skin, nails, all of those outer aspects, she will use them as the expression of her value.

Most notably, young ladies that become strippers and show their bodies for cash can get financially enriched very quickly. But at what expense? The expense of them not having their intimacy private any longer. That is a woman's a glory, it is the mystery of her Maidenhead. To display it for anybody that has $20 is often a way that these ladies found to be able to support themselves, but it's an awful price to pay. Now don't get me wrong this is not a condemnation of those that make those choices. It's just a consideration to begin making better choices. Those types of choices can determine whether or not a woman becomes NOTEWORTHY.

A NOTEWORTHY **Lady** is a woman that has done something of such significance that it causes people to pause and pay attention. That could be because she did something negative, nasty, or not so good. But when it's because she engaged in her very best, that her expectation was met because she was operating from a position of EXCELLENCE, LOVE and GROWTH that allows her to be able to become the ***ELEGANT Lady***.

I don't want this to be a book to be seen as condemning those that have not come to the understanding or the enlightenment of the power of being an ***ELEGANT Lady***. Rather, I wrote it to share that all of us can aspire to that position. That position is NOTEWORTHY. It is NOTEWORTHY to observe that most ***ELEGANT Ladies*** aspire to go higher. Not to allow the Lower Demons to control the situation but instead access to Higher Angels as they reach for a more positive place. The Nattering Nabobs of Negativism are not the ones that will elevate us to the higher heights of what **ELEGANT Ladies** aspire to.

So, in being NOTEWORTHY, the best advice I can give is to make sure that the work you're noted for is worthy of the core values that you've established for yourself. Frequently, women get caught up in circumstances where they react (rather than respond) and make the wrong decision. Often that wrong decision can cause them to lose their resources, lose a relationship, or even lose their freedom. Being intentional allows you to be able to strive toward be Noticed for what is Worthy.

I wasn't the best student in high school. But I was a diligent student that continued to try and was able to elevate from posting passing grades to having decent grades. My focus was to get a diploma, not to get a boyfriend and possibly get pregnant. While most young girls my age were chasing boys or having sleepovers and sharing girl talk, I was focused on the type of future that I wanted to have for myself. So I made sure that I studied hard, and that meant working harder than my peers. Looking back, I think there may have been some undiagnosed cognitive learning issues, but that's not an excuse. I continued to move forward because I had a goal in mind. That goal was to be accepted, to be acknowledged, to be approved, and to be appreciated as a **Young ELEGANT Lady**.

So, that NOTEWORTHY aspiration meant that I had to keep my goals at the top of my mind. Also, I had to have actionable items that I engaged in to help me achieve them. It's easy to point out how the strong man fell, but the difficulty is showing how the weak one rose. No matter what your circumstances, your past, or the issues that you've ever dealt with, you shouldn't use those as reasons to not aspire to become of your highest and best self. They could be the fuel your faith needs to push you to become the woman that you see on the inside. That's a woman that has the potential to change your world and the world of those around you. And that's a NOTEWORTHY *ELEGANT Lady*.

Are you GROWING every day to be received and perceived as an ELEGANT Lady?

1:_____

_____

_____

2:_____

_____

_____

3:_____

_____

_____

4:_____

_____

_____

5:_____

_____

_____

T

TRUSTWORTHY

The last, and perhaps most controversial, letter in the word ***ELEGANT*** is "T" for TRUSTWORTHY. Being TRUSTWORTHY should be an absolute, non-negotiable value. TRUSTWORTHINESS says that people cannot only trust your word, but more importantly, can trust you with their secrets. It also means that you are intentional about delivering what you said you would do.

Too frequently, I see ladies that make bold declarations and proclamations yet end up not being able to deliver. That inability to deliver means that there was an overpromise. The mindset of "under promise and over deliver," means that you observe and assess the situation and give your client, or the person you're talking to, a timeframe that allows you to comfortably be able to complete the task. If you're able to complete the task well ahead of time, then you are seen as being a high performer. If it takes you the amount of time to do it that you promised, you are on time and TRUSTWORTHY.

At the core the word TRUSTWORTHY is the word TRUST. Trust is something that is easy to get, easy to lose, and almost impossible to regain. On the stage of life when a person finds that someone is lying to them, the trust between them becomes nonexistent. When we breach the trust of those that trust in us, it puts us into a position that is untenable. How do we make an account for that trust?

Ordinarily, it would be a matter of taking actions that are congruent with the level of trust that you explain. Often, there are subtleties that don't express themselves in the obvious. It is those times, in those situations and scenarios, that we must be careful. We must be careful that we don't void the trust or take advantage of the trust.

TRUSTWORTHINESS completes the attributes that an **ELEGANT Lady** possesses. As interesting as trust is, it's something that a significant other requires and demands from the person that they have an intimate relationship with. Exhibiting behavior that seeks to deny, destroy, or demean that trust is the reason most relationships are unable to continue.

More importantly, TRUSTWORTHINESS signals to all players involved that this is a person of integrity and honesty, and they can be trusted. How you build that image and mindset of trust is of vital importance. It's not a casual experience that is done overnight. It is something that takes time--the motif of microwaving a cake versus baking it in an oven comes to mind. The ingredients are the same and temperature and heat are applied in some way or form, but when you put a cake in the microwave it comes out as a gooey mess.

But when you take the time to let it marinade... to let it bake in the oven...to let everything come together and become what it was designed to create, then you have a delectable, tasty treat. That's how TRUSTWORTHINESS is in a relationship. Be it man, woman, parent, child, or community where you have placed your trust, it is the ultimate factor in all those scenarios.

One of the worst things in the world is to be confronted with a situation in which your trust has been compromised. Facing the reality that your trust has been breached forces you into a very awkward position. You don't trust the person because they did something to prove that they no longer deserve your trust, yet you are still in the same environment and atmosphere. Your sense of TRUSTWORTHINESS will allow you to endure even that demeaning experience. If you choose to maintain trust and the other person abdicates, it's no indictment on you, your values or who you are. Instead, it's a validation of who you are.

When we consider the aspect of trust, we are believing that the other individual is operating from the same core values that we are. An **ELEGANT Lady** has the core value of EXCELLENCE and LOVE. Not those persons that have no emotions or feelings. Quite the contrary, because she has set standards, she's able to go in and expect that everything will be congruent with those standards.

One of the most egregious things that I had to deal with is men unrelentingly hitting on me. Guys think that because God blessed me a certain way, I'm open to them saying nasty, negative, or non-invited remarks toward me. Nothing is further from the truth. A woman, an **ELEGANT Lady**, does not desire the attention of any man other than her man.

Yet all too often she receives that attention. Guys let their Lower Demons control them and they don't exercise restraint or self-discipline. In all too many cases **ELEGANT Ladies** are getting unrequested undesired attention from many males. This runs the gamut from rude staring to invasion of physical space. A TRUSTWORTHY woman is going to look at the relentless and countless come-ons as inappropriate.

EXCELLENCE, LOVE, EXPECTATION, GROWTH, ATTITUDE, NOTEWORTHINESS, and TRUSTWORTHINESS.

With that as a foundation, an **ELEGANT Lady** can accomplish anything. She's not afraid to go into avenues that her counterparts would consider unsafe, because she has already set the standard of who she is and what she demands from those that she encounters. That's not to say that she isn't intentional about her potential.

So how does one maintain an aura of TRUSTWORTHINESS with so much deceitfulness all around? An **ELEGANT Lady** starts from the posture of TRUSTWORTHINESS, which begins with EXCELLENCE in all the attributes. She uses them as tools in her character-building box to create a castle where her king can be safe. Yes, an **ELEGANT Lady** is someone that a distinguished gentleman will aspire to pursue. Yet all too often the **ELEGANT Lady** finds herself alone. But even during that alone time, she's able to hold onto her values and continue to improve herself. She shall be able to overcome perhaps the greatest cause of failure around lack of patience. And she will remain an **ELEGANT Lady**.

Recap

I just shared with you **7 Key Attributes** that every ***ELEGANT Lady*** needs to possess in order to be able to make progress. I have spent my whole life getting to understand these principles. They are necessary, and women that have acquired them are able to see extraordinary results in their lives. When a woman operates from a spirit of EXCELLENCE, she makes sure that her skincare is hundred percent, and that her hairstyle is appealing. That she's not fad focused and trendy, that they have classic value and long-term applicability. An ***ELEGANT Lady*** looks at life through a lens of LOVE and she's able to forgive and deal with difficult people. But she also understands that she loves herself enough to where she can separate herself from the wrong types of people. An ***ELEGANT Lady*** has an EXPECTANCY that she will have the best, and that she will achieve greater results and reach higher heights.

By doing so she pushes herself and she understands that God has an element involved in that process as well. She does all that she knows to do with **EXCELLENCE** and **LOVE**. Her **EXPECTANCY** believes that the result is going to be good, and that the result leads to her becoming a **GROWTH**-MINDED woman. An **ELEGANT Lady** makes sure that she continues to improve. She continues to grow; she continues to learn, and she continues to take advantage of new technology and new ideas. An **ELEGANT Lady** is never stagnant; instead she has a GROWTH Mindset.

Is important to understand that not only does she have a GROWTH Mindset, but that her **ATTITUDE** is one of victory and continuation. An **ELEGANT Lady** understands that she needs to be **NOTEWORTHY** and **TRUSTWORTHY**. That people will notice that what she is doing is good and want to be a part or invest in it. Trustworthy that they know that investment is something that's going to have a positive return. Those are the attributes of an ***ELEGANT Lady***. Just practicing those 7 **Principles** can open doors that will lead to avenues of revenue and streams of income that are impressive. Thank you and you should consider becoming an ***ELEGANT Lady***.

Take the ELEGANT Lady Test here:

1: How do you display EXCELLENCE?

2: Are you LOVING even if other are not?

3: What are YOUR EXPECTATIONS?

4: What are areas you are showing GROWTH IN?

5: Is you ATTITUDE correct?

6: In what ways are you NOTEWORTHY?

7: Are you TRUSTWORTHY?

About the Author

Lady Jeannette Mack is an Author, Speaker and Entrepreneur. She has been active in the Skincare and haircare industries for over 40 years. Lady Jeannette served as a Clinique Counter Manager at a major Department store for 7 years and has marketed cosmetics, skincare and haircare products independently and online. Jeannette is a Graduate of the ABC schools in San Diego California, majoring in computer competency.

Lady Jeannette helped to facilitate the establishment of the Golden Hills Foursquare Church before relocating to Dallas Texas where she now resides. Lady Mack is the proud mother of three exceptional Adult children and has mentored young ladies at church and nonprofit sessions. She has a thirst for seeing Young Ladies become ELEGANT Ladies!

Made in the USA
Columbia, SC
15 September 2022